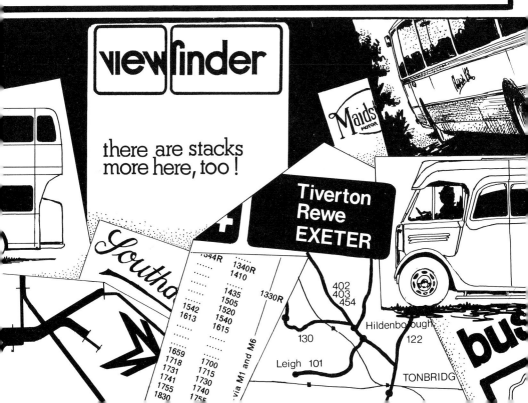

a London RF album

London Transport & London Country
RF buses & coaches in their later years

photographed & described by
Ray Stenning & Trevor Whelan

Ray Stenning, 'brought up' on RLHs & GSs,
first discovered the RF on family shopping trips
to Croydon by Green Line. These must have
had a lasting impression for he has observed,
pursued, travelled on & photographed London's
RFs with affection and respect since, and many
other buses besides. A designer & artist, he
paints a complete picture by understanding
their background & development and relating
them to their environment, necessary to
communicate what he feels to be their character.

Trevor Whelan, a devoted follower of many
forms of transport, shares this enthusiasm for
a classic vehicle. His encounters with the RF
brought him into close contact with the type
over a large sphere of operation. An emphasis on
the final years is one of sincere respect yet
seemingly casual observance, qualities Trevor
uses with great skill to make his statement
about the RF in all its forms.

artwork, layout & design by Ray Stenning/Viewfinder

typesetting by Rockwell Printers, Wellington
in 8pt Gill Sans

copyright 1977

viewfinder

75 North Street
Wellington
Somerset TA21 8NA

ISBN 0 906051 00 2   Printed by Acanthus Press, Wellington, Somerset.

London's buses are famous the world over and, superficially at least arouse more interest than those from elsewhere. Strange to recount but the most heralded have always been double-deckers and usually red at that! Very few followers of road passenger transport haven't heard of the K, NS, the RT or the Routemaster. London's single-deckers have achieved lesser degrees of fame, more often than not through technical innovation or novelty such as the side-engined Q or early underfloor-engined TF. The conventional T class AEC Regals were certainly numerous and well loved but their introduction was spread across the years from 1929 when the first entered LGOC and Green Line fleets to 1948 when the last were put on the road. Even though Ts could be found in Central red, in Country green and Green Line service, there were so many different versions—different bodies and different chassis Marks—that the only common factor was the class designation.

This was not the case with the RF. Based on AEC's underfloor-engined Regal Mk IV chassis, some 700 examples quickly entered service over three brief years from 1951 to 1953 and stayed around for the following quarter of a century, a feat of endurance unanticipated at the time. Apart from the first 25 built to the old maximum permissible length of 27'6" and with roof observation panels, all were virtually identical in appearance. Minor details naturally distinguished Green Line coaches, but the entire class more or less represented the philosophy of standardisation with all its advantages and drawbacks.

It is this embodiment of a concept taken to a logical conclusion—the RF in its time was London's only full size single-decker (the RFW & GS classes fulfilled special needs and were in a minority anyway—GSs were eventually replaced by RFs on most duties)—and the sheer longevity of the class that makes such robust vehicles something to be remembered for.

There are other books that give you a history of the RF—that isn't our intention here, although certain historical facts are mentioned in the words used to complement the pictures, especially in respect of certain unusual batches and the brilliant rejuvenation given by Misha Black to the Green Line fleet in the mid-sixties. No, this book compiled with fondness and flair by two dedicated enthusiasts, is a reflection on how we came to know, observe, to love and even live the RF in its many forms and many faces during later years in London service. It is a collection, a recollection, of many memories distilled in photographic form. None is earlier than 1964 and the newest taken in 1977. As a visual tribute it is ambiguous, for it is unashamedly sentimental and ruthlessly objective. A dirty RF is as deserving of love as a clean one.

The album hopefully captures through our eyes the character and many moods of this handsome type in service, at home or wherever we happened to see it. The rural bus plodding along leafy lanes, the commuter bus plying busy, bustling town routes, the Green Line coach (well, only just coach!) supplying useful links across and around the Metropolis. Some of the locations may feature prominently and there are glaring omissions of what for many might be more typical of the RF. We make no apology since, as we said, it is a subjective tribute to how WE saw the RF. We hope you like our view but more importantly we hope we have done justice to these magnificent buses—after a quarter of a century on the streets they deserve an album to themselves!

Ray Stenning

Trevor Whelan

1

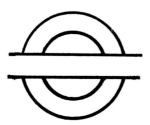

. . . in Green Line garb

RFs will be best remembered for their sterling Green Line work. Twenty years of daily journeying, mostly from far flung corners of London's bus network across the capital to equally distant destinations—Tunbridge Wells to Windsor, Dorking to Luton, Aylesbury to Westerham for example. Taking people to work and home again, for shopping in town or a day in the country, Green Line was a household word and to most people inseparable from the RFs that so faithfully worked them.

During those years spanning the hopeful fifties and swinging sixties into the glum seventies RF coaches wore a variety of faces. Perhaps the most familiar that shown here—black roof boards (previously dark green) with orange lettering, and the Green Line bulls eye motif with route number on a black background to the left of an orange blind. Maybe it's just that my first recollection of RF coaches was of this type. Either way they adopted this guise from about 1957 to the mid-sixties, so it was the longest lasting.

Apart from some of the Aldgate based routes, every Green Line service was maintained by RF coaches during this period until Routemasters entered the scene after 1962 and even then the RF still predominated for many years.

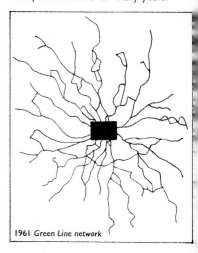

1961 *Green Line network*

Dorking could boast three Green Line routes to London and beyond when this picture was taken in 1966. (*below*) RF 228 leaves the bus station, also its home garage forecourt, for the long 714 trip to Luton. In compensation for the lost 712 and 713 south of London a new 703 from Dorking to London only was tried. Failing to sustain custom it disappeared too, leaving the 714 alone to serve Dorking.

London's first Green Line route not to traverse central London was introduced in July 1953, southern peripheral 725 linking Gravesend with Bromley, Croydon, Kingston and Windsor. Successful from the word go, RFs like RF 30 (DT), seen here leaving West Croydon bus station (*upper right*) bound for Windsor, worked it until striking Alexander bodied Swifts (SMA) arrived in 1971, a diverted NBC order from South Wales.

The familiar tale of falling traffic during the sixties led to several Green Line casualties. Route 710 lost, typically its southern section first, later the entire length. RF 178 (MA) at its southern terminus, Crawley bus station (*lower right*), before plying the still intact route in 1966 to Chesham.

Green Line destination blinds were given a brighter look in the mid-sixties, cleaner lettering on a yellow background without the familiar bulls-eye (GREEN LINE appeared yellow in a black strip along the top of the display). This was just a prelude to a major updating of the Green Line image, now beginning to jade a little—RFs had been diligently performing coach duties for 15 years, remember!

Misha Black was called in to revamp them and his brilliantly skillful modernising applied to RF 136 in 1966. The rest followed suit throughout 1966/7 injecting a needed lift to the Green Line RF image. A much bolder, sharper livery style was used in conjunction with many design modifications. Roof boards changed to yellow to match the crisp new livery and blinds.

. . . a new face

With a regal blow from its exhaust, RF 167 (HH) speeds smokily away from Godstone roundabout on a southbound 708 in 1966 (*top left*). It shows the newer blind with the old livery. In contrast, pulling away from Godstone garage less than a year later on the same working, is modernised RF 109 (*lower left*). Amazing the difference made to the frontal look by the curved driver's screen and twin headlamps. RMCs took over the 708 from late '67 but RFs returned in 1969.

The 707 faded out in 1969 but it is worth noting that the number was never shown on roof boards due to interworking with the 706—instead they simply read '. . . Westerham or Oxted'. RF 184 (TG), old livery new blinds, at Titsey Corner, Limpsfield (*top right*) offers comparison with modernised RFs 181 and 46 at Hurst Green (*lower right*). These winter and summer views were on a SuO 707 extension covering withdrawn Sunday 464 buses, a facility lasting only from 1965–8. The scene is identical with that on page 11.

. . . in far corners

Stansted Airport is the furthest NE point of the Green Line web, served by the 720 from Aldgate. RF 45 (HA) in bus colours in 1975 (*above*) with appropriate hardware in the background!

The 704 reaches out beyond the Country area at Tonbridge to Tunbridge Wells, a hangover from Autocar days. RF 141 (DG) on the final leg of the journey at Tonbridge Station (*left*) compares with modernised RF 50 (WR) at the purpose built Tunbridge Wells terminus (*below*). TW, closed in 1967, supplied only the 704, by that time RCL operated.

A northern counterpart to the 725 came about in 1966, RF worked 724 from Romford to High Wycombe. The first one-man-operated Green Line service, its Express route swept a broad arc away from London's suburbs to serve Harlow, Hertford, St Albans and Watford.

Just a year later another cross-country route started. Express 727, again OMO, linked Crawley and Gatwick Airport to Heathrow Airport, Watford Junction and Luton, providing an amazing range of connections between air, rail and other road services. Initially RF operated, members of the RC class later took over but their unreliability caused RFs to appear on many duties. From December 1971 new RP coaches became its preserve, displaced RFs moving to the 724. To strengthen the road/rail/air bias of these two routes, 727 was extended to Luton Airport during 1971 and 724 diverted to run to Heathrow and Staines, rather than High Wycombe, in 1972.

A well loaded RF 87 (ST), with London Country logo but minus roof boards, works an eastbound 724 at Harlow Bus Station in 1974. (above)

From the outset the 727 has had constantly high loadings. Soon after introduction in 1967 a 727 waits to leave Crawley. (lower right) RF 70 (RG) was one of several modernised RFs downseated to 35 by fitting extra luggage racks at the rear, for the benefit of air passengers, as seen in the interior view of RF 79 (right). Also to cope with this gruelling service engines were uprated and larger fuel tanks fitted.

Pottering on rural backwaters, moving the masses in the new towns or working important between town routes, the Country RF was part of London's bus scene for practically a quarter of a century—a staggering feat!

They could be seen in every corner of the system, hurrying or sauntering, loaded or light—at Guildford and Hertford, Sevenoaks and St Albans, in new towns like Stevenage or old villages like Shere. Together with 84 small capacity GSs delivered in 1953 they upheld every single-deck green bus route and eventually extended OMO to them all.

They worked the long 434 through three counties—four if you count East & West Sussex separately—linking Edenbridge in Kent with Horsham in W Sussex (for some years only to Crawley) taking in Surrey at Dormansland (see page 26) and E Sussex at East Grinstead. Coming over Troy Town railway bridge, more rural than its name might suggest, is RF 558 (CY) on a loop to the Edenbridge end (top left).

Worked by Addlestone's RFs the 427/437/456 joined the Weybridge area to Woking. One of my first memories of a bus RF was at Byfleet on these routes. Much later, in 1967, as storm clouds gather RF 651 (WY) sets out from its home garage (top right).

Once GS operated, route 481 eventually succumbed to RFs like 687 (LH) at Epsom Station (middle right). Back in Kent and a few miles north of Edenbridge, RF 615 (CM) takes on passengers at Crockham Hill (lower right). Shiny from a fresh coat of paint this, as the others on this page, represents the standard single-deck Country bus of London Transport days. Externally they closely resembled the Green Line version before modernisation, the main difference being LT transfers, cream window surrounds and no roof boards.

. . . in Country colours

Autumn 1962 saw a number of country routes changed from GS to RF operation, using RFs displaced from Green Line work by new double-deck Routemaster (RMC) coaches then entering service. Whether by design or by accident some of these demoted coaches were reverting to bus work, having started their lives as such.

Renumbering in 1956 also involved increasing the Green Line fleet. RF 289–294 were converted from 41-seat central area buses and 295–313 from 41-seat country buses. This involved rearrangement of the forward seating layout to conform with Green Line standards, but because of their closer seat spacing in bus form the front offside inward facing seat had room for two (original coaches had a single seat) and its corresponding nearside transverse seat had more than generous legroom.

Ribbed wooden flooring was replaced by a composite material and inside roof luggage racks fitted, allowing for the removal of seat stanchion poles. These racks differed from those on conventional coaches, which were of integral pattern, in that they had an obvious 'added' look and didn't extend so far rearwards.

On return to bus work little was done to the interior save equipping them for OMO and later replacing the front nearside seat with a luggage pen.

. . . back in Country colours

Externally they remained much as before but now sported bus transfers and cream window surrounds. Roof brackets fitted for carrying traditional Green Line destination boards remained in position. RF 309 pioneered the reconversion, all in the range 298–313 becoming buses again.

Chelsham's more than adequate allocation of GSs were ousted by six RFs, including unique-liveried 313. She had been one of several Green Lines painted in an experimental light green main body colour in 1961. This she carried through to bus days for a few months, now of course with cream window surrounds and thus was the sole RF to wear this not unpleasing hybrid colour scheme.

CM's initial quota of RF buses were all of this type. On overhaul they became dispersed to other garages and bodies swopped. RF 310 for example received a standard bus body and went to neighbouring EG. She is seen in this form (*top left*) on a local route in East Grinstead. On the other hand RF 553 had its standard bus body replaced by one of these modified versions when it came to CM after overhaul in 1966, shown (*lower left*) picking up by Oxted Police Station on the 464. Also on a 464 working, RF 308 in sunshine at Hurst Green in 1965. (*top right*) Shortly afterwards she was sent to Harlow and spent much of her remaining days there until withdrawal in 1972. Interior views of 312 in later bus form complete the record.

11

Broxbourne Station is served by frequent electric trains from Liverpool Street and by single-deck London Country 392/393 between Welwyn & Harlow—also 327 until withdrawal in 1977. RF 302 (HA), of the batch described on the previous page (*top left*) contrasts its traditional livery style with modernised RF 45 (*lower left*) in August 1975.

National style roof fleet names started to appear with the National livery, as can be seen on RF 613 (GR) outside Garston, displaying a 352 blind (*top right*). The practice of showing full route information on the rear blind was discontinued some years ago.

In contrast at Windsor in April 1977 is still the old order (*lower right*). Lincoln green with yellow lining on RF 251 (WR) working coincidentally a 452, with a rear-engined Merlin in front. The RF rear end is more attractive, wouldn't you agree?

.. in LONDON COUNTRY colours

A variety of liveries were worn by LCBS RF buses. At takeover from London Transport in 1970 Lincoln green with cream relief was still standard. Gold LONDON COUNTRY fleet names in plain capitals without underlining replaced the well known LT ones. These were later changed to canary yellow, a refreshing bright shade that gradually, but not totally, supplanted cream as relief colour too, following experiments a year or two earlier.

Adverts were appearing in the usual mid-panel fleet name position on some RF buses, which meant the bus either went unlegended or had the name removed to a non-standard position, sometimes to good effect! (*see page 31*).

Unkindly but accurately dubbed the 'flying polo', London Country's unhappy symbol seen elsewhere in this book—nice enough on its own—perhaps borrowed too heavily from the LT bulls-eye to be a clear graphic success. It was applied to

buses, coaches, buildings & publicity rapidly (LT bulls-eyes were removed even more rapidly, first!) but the all-conquering National corporate identity soon laid it to rest.

Before unrelieved National leaf green was adopted some hybrid liveries occurred and remained to the last. An intermediate lighter green was tried—first appearing on new AF one-man double-deckers in 1971—but somehow the impact of canary yellow against it was less dramatic. As further modernised RFs were demoted to buses, due to arriving new coaches under London Country's vehicle replacement programme, they brought a whole range of unusual livery styles to the fleet.—Lincoln green or light green with yellow, leaf green with white, without white.

All in all the post-LT Country bus scene was rather colourful!

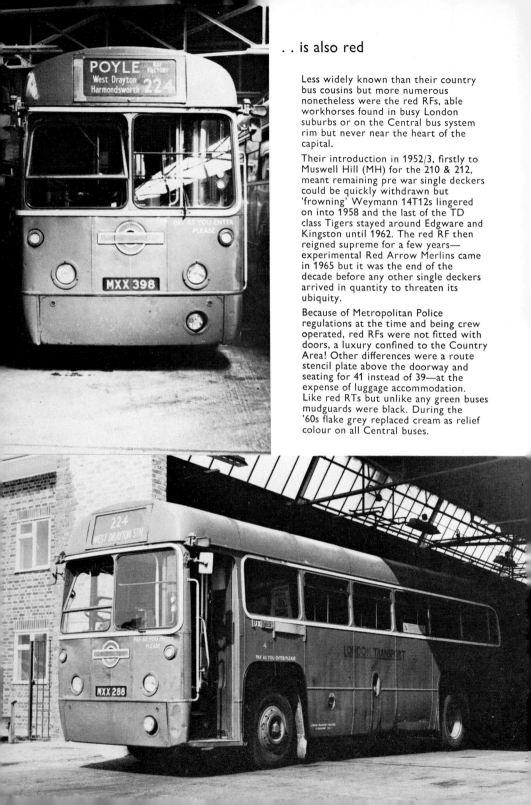

. . is also red

Less widely known than their country bus cousins but more numerous nonetheless were the red RFs, able workhorses found in busy London suburbs or on the Central bus system rim but never near the heart of the capital.

Their introduction in 1952/3, firstly to Muswell Hill (MH) for the 210 & 212, meant remaining pre war single deckers could be quickly withdrawn but 'frowning' Weymann 14T12s lingered on into 1958 and the last of the TD class Tigers stayed around Edgware and Kingston until 1962. The red RF then reigned supreme for a few years— experimental Red Arrow Merlins came in 1965 but it was the end of the decade before any other single deckers arrived in quantity to threaten its ubiquity.

Because of Metropolitan Police regulations at the time and being crew operated, red RFs were not fitted with doors, a luxury confined to the Country Area! Other differences were a route stencil plate above the doorway and seating for 41 instead of 39—at the expense of luggage accommodation. Like red RTs but unlike any green buses mudguards were black. During the '60s flake grey replaced cream as relief colour on all Central buses.

One man operation, widespread on single deckers elsewhere, didn't come to London's red buses until November 1964 though some Central RFs (502–538) had been equipped for OMO as early as 1959. As such they at last received air operated folding doors, rightfully theirs, and a luggage pen like the standard Country version which reduced seating capacity to 39. OMO spread rapaciously thereafter and by 1972 all red RFs still in service were of this type. Two man operation by single deckers seems almost unthinkable in the late 1970s!

Famous at Kingston and Uxbridge (see following pages), they were also known to many for their work on the 210 from Golders Green over Hampstead Heath with a tight spot at The Spaniards, and the 227 in the Crystal Palace/Bromley area, also once boasting a tight spot through Chislehurst Arch until demolition in 1963. 227 was one of the last crew RF routes.

In whatever location they were found their fine proportions could only have resulted from LT's excellent design standards, applied to everything from posters & publicity to buses & buildings —like Arnos Grove Underground station (top right), with RF 504 on a 251 on 22nd January 1977, the last Saturday of RF operation at EW.

Red RFs undergoing maintenance inside UX and FW (right), and outside UX (left).

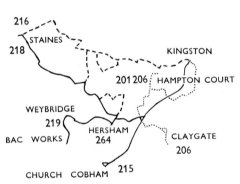

. . . at Kingston

Kingston's (K) interest is in its long established network of suburban single-deck routes, some shared with Fulwell (FW), fanning westwards into semi-countryside as the 215 to Church Cobham, as the 219 through affluent housing of the strockbroker belt to Weybridge, or following the Thames as the 218 to Staines.

Once the haunt of ageing Ts or LTs, some with rebuilt bodywork,—weak Walton bridge kept these longer than otherwise should have been—several ex-Green Line Ts & Country Area Qs had been painted red and worked from Kingston in the early '50s before RFs took charge for the next twenty years. For a while K was the only all single-deck garage.

Country Area 418 penetrated Kingston's red domain along with the 406 up from Reigate. National liveried RF 567 (LH) surrounded at Kingston Station (*lower right*), unusually substituting for a newer single-decker.

Hounslow (AV) operated RFs, notably on the 237 through Feltham & Shepperton to once almost rural Chertsey Station. This was an early conversion to OMO. RF 360 outside the garage in 1965 (*top left*), and RF 428 at Chertsey Station in early 1977 (*lower left*).

Permanent transfers denoting a one-man bus replaced removable slip boards with the spread of this method of operation.

In eastern suburbs the red RF found a home at garages such as Romford (NS) Loughton (L) & Enfield (E).

A mile or so from the 121 terminus at Enfield Town RF 533 (E) heads along Southbury Road, Ponders End, in April 1976 (*top right*). Ponders End garage, 533's home then, can be seen on the right, officially known as Enfield.

On the same day RF 506 (E) in Southbury Road changes drivers whilst working a 121 from Enfield to Chingford Station (*lower right*). Both rear indicators used to be found above the numberplate on the offside. A simple modification lead to a less confusing system.

... out west, out east

The entrance on the RF is narrow in comparison with more modern single-deck buses but the clear design detail makes it inviting. RF 526 shows its pay-as-you-enter notices outside and on the driver's door, so there should be no mistake. (*top far left*)

RF 400's non-standard modern doors (*top left*). Standard RF doors had two glass panels in each leaf. Semaphore indicators were fitted to some RFs for a while and the position can be seen to the rear of the door. The flashing indicator 'ears' had flexible mountings for obvious reasons.

The attention to detail that has always distinguished London's buses was quite often cleverly executed. The bulls-eye symbol prominently yet finely displayed on the front of RF vehicles was hinged in the middle (*middle left*). Let this down and it would reveal the radiator filler cap!

A modernised Green Line RF interior (*below left*). The sturdy and elegant appearance belies its date of origin. These versions carried a well conceived colour scheme of maroon, silver grey and off white. Fluorescent lighting brightened the interior also. A message on the bulkhead urges smokers to occupy rear seats yet ashtrays are provided all the way forward!

A standard Country Bus interior, virtually identical to red buses after conversion to OMO (*top right*). Obvious differences from the coach version are the lack of luggage racks and consequent grab poles, ribbed wooden flooring and extra longitudinal seats. Nevertheless the same attention to detail and sturdy construction is evident.

Route 473 is mentioned and illustrated on page 26 at its 'country' terminus. Then as here the starting point was Crawley, where RF 548 (CY) was photographed in 1965 (*below right*).

London Transport and its successor London Country benefitted well from establishment of the new towns during the fifties and on through the sixties. As well as Crawley it had Hemel Hempstead, Stevenage & Harlow in its operating area, and RFs maintained many of the town routes in these places during their time.

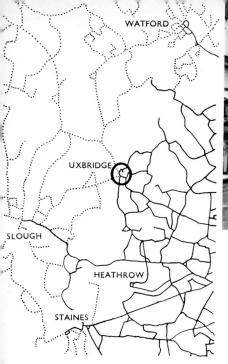

. . . in Uxbridge

Uxbridge, as shown on the map, is on the border between London Transport & London Country. Green buses trail northwards to Hemel Hempstead, Watford and beyond, and work across from Windsor and Slough. Demoted from Green Line work, London Country RF buses from WR are seen here plying the 458 which also serves Iver and Langley.

Uxbridge (UX) was one of the last outposts of the red RF, operating such routes as the 223 from Ruislip to Heathrow Airport and the 224 from Uxbridge to Laleham, just beyond Staines. RFs 452 & 524, with equally coincidental permutations on their registration figures (MXX 429, MLL 942!) are busy in and around the focus of the town's bus operations, Uxbridge LT Station, working the 223.

. . . in Limpsfield village

Limpsfield lies below the North Downs, close to Oxted and just in Surrey. For many years non-standard double deckers (famous 'Godstone' STLs & RLHs) and small single deckers (Cubs then GSs) were its mainstay.

It was Green Line 707 that first brought the RF in 1952, touching a corner of the village on its way out of Oxted—shown here one Sunday morning in 1966 by RF 125 (*above*) turning towards Titsey Hill. In pre-RF days this formidable climb required coaches with a special back axle ratio.

With the 707 no longer to keep it company (it went in 1969), London Country RF 154 (CM) hastens its lightly loaded 465 past St Peter's (*lower left*).

A 465 in more prosperous days (*top right*)—1966 and RF 623 (CM) in Spring sunshine leaves behind the busy A25 to strike across open commonland. In 1973 at exactly the same spot, the same bus as shown opposite is this time glimpsed through trees bordering the golf course heading a 464 to Westerham (*lower right*).

Drastic revisions a couple of years later removed the 465 as such and stopped the 464 short at The Chart, just 2 miles on from this part of the Common. CM's RFs had already been replaced by short, narrow Bristol BNs by then.

. . . on Limpsfield Common

. . . outside Inns

The Plough at Dormansland

In a leafy corner of Surrey, not far from the Kent border in one direction and close to the Sussex boundary in the other, The Plough at Dormansland has seen buses come and go since 1924.

RF 579 (*above*) working a 434 from Edenbridge in 1966 hurries past RF 310 (EG), itself occupying layover time outside the inn on route 428. The history of RF 310 is outlined elsewhere in this book.

The unusual and extremely clear all lower-case destination screen layout is well displayed by RF 551, fresh from overhaul in 1965. (*upper left*)

A 434 variation, numbered 473, was introduced in 1952. Demoted from Green Line duties, RF 42 (*lower left*) leaves for Crawley one Saturday evening in 1966.

. . . The Golden Lion

Despite being two thirds of the way along Hoddesdon High Street already, RF 554 (HG) is only just entering the town centre, an imaginary boundary marked by the Golden Lion. In this July 1976 view she is working a 393 short—Hertford Bus Station/Broxbourne Station/Hertford, Horns Mill—the only such working of the day. This early morning journey also ran on Saturdays but with amended timings.

From the January 1977 timetable, following the 327 withdrawal, these journeys were covered by 392 workings to Nazeing Village (see page 33).

. . . in place of trains

Weekends are often the only time for essential engineering work on the railways. If services are suspended then buses have to be substituted. Track relaying between Lingfield and East Grinstead on a succession of Sundays in 1968 brought on this occasion (*above*) RF 623 & 568 (RG) to supply a temporary bus link, seen outside Lingfield Station. An interesting feature of this operation was a taxi service from and to the intermediate station of Dormans connecting with the line of route at Felcourt, little used but mandatory!

RF 648 (HG) turning into Stanstead Road, Hoddesdon, on a similar duty one Sunday in February 1975 (*below*). The temporary link here was between Broxbourne and Hertford East.

ngineering Wor

A connecting bu
will be provided
& East Grinstea
trains. British R
delay to your jou

esdown

Upper Warlingham

Woldin

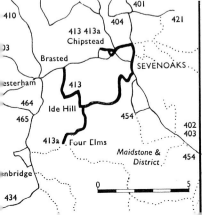

. . . over the hills of Kent

Just below the tortuous A25 between Westerham and Sevenoaks the landscape, heavily wooded with beech and pine, rises steadily and then suddenly plunges 500 feet into hopfields and orchards of the Kentish Weald. Out from Sevenoaks 413 & 413a used to run to Ide Hill on the edge of the escarpment. The 413 turned northward, still in magnificent woodland to Brasted, while the infrequent 413a dropped down to Four Elms, a tiny village more used to M & D buses on their way to and from Edenbridge or Tunbridge Wells.

In late afternoon sun on a 413a short, RF 692 (DG) has just turned at Ide Hill to return to Sevenoaks and Chipstead (top). By 1968 the 413a's days were numbered. RF 239 (DG) loses its only passenger at journey's end, Four Elms (lower).

29

. . . bus passing coach

Modernised Green Line RF 281 (WY) picking up passengers for Woking is overtaken by red bus RF 545 (K) in Kingston (*above*). Studio 7 beyond the bus station used to be called Kingston Kinema. (*see page 16*).

Country RF 598 (CM) performs a similar action to then recently modernised RF 181 (TG) at its terminus in Oxted (*below*). Note the better proportioned and repositioned bulls-eye, also the repositioned sidelamps, indicators and number plate.

Buses often have to be substituted for coaches due to breakdowns or extra traffic, even in the best run concerns. Whether good or bad, in the case of RFs the difference is less distinct.

RF 197 (RG), formerly a Green Line coach, a bus here, slips down Reigate Hill near the end of its 711 journey (*top right*) from High Wycombe in the mid-sixties.

At the close of RF's Green Line days when new vehicles were in short supply RF buses frequently made forays on coach routes. With its broad waist band now bright yellow, RF 49 (HG) at the Hertford terminus of the SO 715A from Guildford in 1975 (*middle right*).

The daily 715 avoids Kingston by using the by-pass. RF 285 outside HG garage (*below*) shows a very non-standard fleet name position! Several RF buses were fitted with reduced blind displays because of the multiplicity of workings and the need to accomodate all routes operated.

. bus in place of coach

... bus that was coach

A shrinking Green Line network and arrival of newer coaches caused many RFs to be demoted to local bus work from the early '60s onwards, as these examples show.

RF 78 (HG) in Rye Park, Hoddesdon on the 327 in August 1974 (*top left*).

RF 92 (CY) at a long established stand in the old part of Crawley (*left*). Circular 426 was one of the last routes to be operated by the RFs' immediate predecessors, the 15T13 Regal Mk III Ts, right up until 1962!

With a lean to port RF 226 (EG) in East Grinstead High Street (*below*).

A muddy lane draped with willows in Nazeing. RF 212 (HG) at the end of its days in 1977 is all that's needed to complete this winter scene (*opposite*). On an early morning 392 short, replacing the 327, the improvised blind display lends poignancy to a never to be repeated occurrence.

Pay a
Fares r

. . . rural ride

Trundling along half-forgotten country lanes the 494 served isolated settlements between East Grinstead, Lingfield & Oxted from 1948 to 1973. In its early days a rear-engined CR was often used but RFs worked the increasingly infrequent timetable for the last 9 years before loss of local authority grants caused its total demise.

RF 59 at Crowhurst Lane End one summer Saturday in 1966 (above). The bus, demoted from coach work by now, is turning towards Tandridge and about to pass under a railway bridge carrying the near straight Redhill-Tonbridge line.

Just a few months before 494's disappearance from the bus map, NBC liveried RF 226 waits at Oxted Station terminus (below). In part compensation local routes were modified to serve Tandridge and in Lingfield, and a Postbus started from Oxted to Lingfield using many roads once travelled by the 494.

RF 303 (EG), of the batch described on page 10, also at CM first, often worked the 494 (opposite lower) but is seen here in East Grinstead Bus Station on town route 435 in 1965.

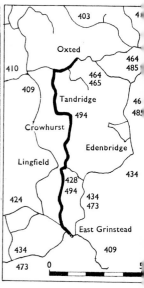

34

...Green Line failure and success

An unsuccessful bid to retain traffic on the 709 was made by incorporating an express section. It only lasted a year and was in operation when RF 47 (MA) was seen arriving at Godstone in 1965 (*above*). Later the route only operated south of London and from 1967, when RCLs were in charge, just during peak hours.

Every year since 1966 Green Line 706 has been seasonally extended to Chartwell with great success. Modernised RF 65 (TG) at Chartwell in 1967 (*right*).

36

. . . going

At the takeover by London Country Bus Services of the country area system on 1st Jan 1970 green RF strength was amazingly still nearly 550. Over the next few years massive inroads were made into their ranks producing the situation in Autumn 1976 of just 44 (though LT still had 124 in stock), many of them awaiting disposal as in this line up at HG in 1975 (*top right*). RF 651 is seen in better days on page 9.

LCBS found further use themselves for 3 former buses in 1973. RF 556 & 647 became towing vehicles in a distinctive light grey with yellow livery. 647 is shown at Windsor and inside WR (*left*). Note its purposeful interior.

RF 594's role was to become that of recruiting vehicle in July of 1973, initially in an all leaf green colour scheme bearing the fleet legend 'LONDON COUNTRY NEEDS YOU'. Later it received the more striking livery shown here (*centre right*), resting out of use at DS in January 1977. Detail modifications were also carried out.

Despite outside sales and these further 'in house' uses many RFs were simply time expired and befell the undignified fate of RF 267 (*below right*), forlorn outside Staines (ST) in April 1976.

Many RFs sold have seen further service with other concerns—Premier Travel of Cambridge operated several including some of the ex-private hire versions. Schools and clubs have provided a ready market, a compliment to the RFs' strength and sound design.

BEA took some for use as airside coaches at Heathrow, including RF 273 as long ago as 1964. 10 years later it was caught many miles distant at Othery, Somerset with a car transporter (below), most attractively finished and lined out. Note the extra lamps and AEC badge.

Halls of Hounslow operated several ex-Country RFs under their Silverline banner as transfer buses also at Heathrow. Ex-RF 665 had already been sold by Halls when photographed in March 1975 (above).

... not gone

RF 10 restored to her original green and grey looks resplendent at Weymouth Bus Rally in 1974. She has collected a number of trophies since preservation—just look at the boards on display!

Originally the first twenty five RFs were for the private hire fleet and built to a short length of 27ft 6ins. In 1956 RF 16–25 were put to ordinary Green Line work and repainted accordingly. All twenty five had been withdrawn before the time-span dealt with in this book, but it is pertinent to mention that the private hire examples (RF 1–15) succumbed to a rather drab all green livery in their last years under London Transport ownership.

... remembered

in other books

Much of the information in this book can only be described as knowledge acquired through experience, observation or incidental inquisitive research! We have referred to other books for certain facts both intentionally and accidentally and where this has been the case we gratefully acknowledge those sources, too numerous to mention individually even if we could identify them specifically.

What we can do, however, is to draw your attention to just some of the many books and publications that have been and are available if you want to know more about London's buses, particularly the RF.

London's Single-deck Bus of the Fifties	by J S Wagstaff Oakwood Press Locomotive Paper 101 Story of the RF, RFW & GS classes, & BEA coaches.
also in the same series	
5 The London Motor Bus 1896–1968	by R W Kidner
42 The London Country Bus	
57 The London RT Bus	
83 The London Routemaster Bus	all by J S Wagstaff
abc London Buses	An illustrated fleet list of LT/LCBS published over the years by Ian Allan. 1977 edition is the 32nd.
also from Ian Allan	
London Buses in Camera 1933–1969	By John A Gray
London's Suburban Buses	by John A Gray
London Bus & Tram Album (out of print)	by V H Darling
Buses Annual	A yearly production since 1964, this usually has some topic to do with London.
London Transport Buses	from Capital Transport An illustrated fleet list.
London Transport Scrapbook for 1975	from Capital Transport
The London Motor Bus	
The Story of the London Bus	both from London Transport
A History of London Transport	2 volumes published by Allen & Unwin
The London RLH by P Gascoine	A complete history of London's post-war lowbridge bus.
London Bus Review of 1973	These yearly reviews by the London Omnibus
1974	Traction Society are fully illustrated, fully
1975	comprehensive studies of both vehicles &
1976	services of LT & LCBS over the previous year.

The London Omnibus Traction Society has a large selection of other publications about London's buses and bus services and their quarterly *London Bus Magazine* is strongly recommended for its interesting, informative articles about London Transport and London Country subjects old and new, its topicality and high quality.

Buses is an Ian Allan monthly that few enthusiasts haven't heard of. Virtually required reading it has a regular London column and fleet news of London Country. *Buses Extra* is a quarterly offshoot of this dealing with particular themes more closely.

The PSV Circle & Omnibus Society have published many items of London interest, including *Fleet History of the T Class*, but one just can't do justice to their comprehensive range in such a short space.

Then there are the Viewfinder books.

Various models are available of London buses including an excellent 4mm scale white metal kit from GS Models of the RF.

Do you know something about buses we don't ?

.... if you do, then the publishers would like to hear from you. Maybe you're an expert on some bus topic or perhaps your photograph collection has something to make it worthy of further exposure. No matter how much of a specialist interest you feel your 'thing' to be, it could well fascinate others.

Drop us a line and maybe your subject will help Viewfinder be a bit more of the bus scene seen!